Place

IRA
WORDWORTHY

by
Stephen Cosgrove
illustrated by
Wendy Edelson

MULTNOMAH

Other books in this series
Fiddler
Shadow Chaser
Gossamer
Derby Downs
T.J. Flopp

IRA WORDWORTHY
© 1989 by Stephen Cosgrove
Published by Multnomah Press
Portland, Oregon 97266

Printed in the United States of America

Library of Congress Cataloging-in-Publication Data

Cosgrove, Stephen.
    Ira Wordworthy / by Stephen Cosgrove ; illustrated by
Wendy Edelson
        p. cm.
    Summary: The badger proprietor of a country store, who
fusses and fumes at the boys and girls that sit on his steps
to read, changes his attitude entirely when young Rita Raccoon
discovers his secret shortcoming and remedies it.
    ISBN 0-88070-279-6
    [1. Reading—Fiction. 2. Animals—Fiction.] I. Title.
PZ7.C8187Ir   1989
[E]—dc20
                                        89-3175
                                        CIP
                                        AC

90 91 92 93 94 95 96 97 - 10 9 8 7 6 5 4 3 2

In the United States today there are over twenty seven million adults who are functionally illiterate. Many Americans cannot read a newspaper, or enjoy a book, or even follow the instructions on a job application. They have never found the magic of words and the delightful pictures that can be painted with them. We want to help teach these people to read, which is why we're sending the proceeds from this book to literacy organizations around the country. In the meantime, we hope the children who will read *Ira Wordworthy* will understand how special the gift of literacy is for everyone.

We thank you for sharing Ira's story and his inspiration. Together, we can keep the joys of reading alive.

Peter H. Coors

Stephen Cosgrove

Coors Foundation For Family Literacy.

Farther than far
and to the very edge
of the horizon was a
path bordered in lacy
fern. If you walked down
that path in search of lost
hopes and dreams you would
find a land called Barely There.

Barely There . . . a land where old fat owls tell
stories true, and laugh and laugh but never at you.
Barely There . . . where dreams swirl and twist
with clouds that fly, and the morning mist
seems to sigh . . . Barely There . . .
Barely There.

If you followed that path as it twisted and turned, at first you might feel lost, but the deeper you went the more you would find that it all began to look oh, so familiar. If you followed it farther still, the twisting path would turn into a softly rutted, red-clay road.

Things were a bit more organized here; plants were planted in orderly rows of corn, wheat, and barley. Houses sat back from the dusty road with shutters drawn and porches swept clean. Woodchucks, gophers, and old guinea hens plowed and tended the fields that blended with nature's wondrous bounty.

The dusty, red-clay road wound through fields and clusters of cabins and cottages, past the school with its rusty old bell, and ended at the absolute center of the land of Barely There. It was here, at the edge of this tiny town square, that the only store stood—WORDWORTHY'S FEED, SEED, AND MERCANTILE.

Three worn, rickety steps up and you were on the porch where barrels and boxes of seeds became chairs and benches. An old screen door screech-creaked open and crash-slammed shut as outside walked an old gray badger dressed in a starched white shirt, a black bow tie, and a crisp, clean apron tied 'round his chubby waist.

This was Ira Wordworthy, the proprietor of the mercantile, who always swept his porch with a bundled broom of hazel hay as the sun came up to greet the day.

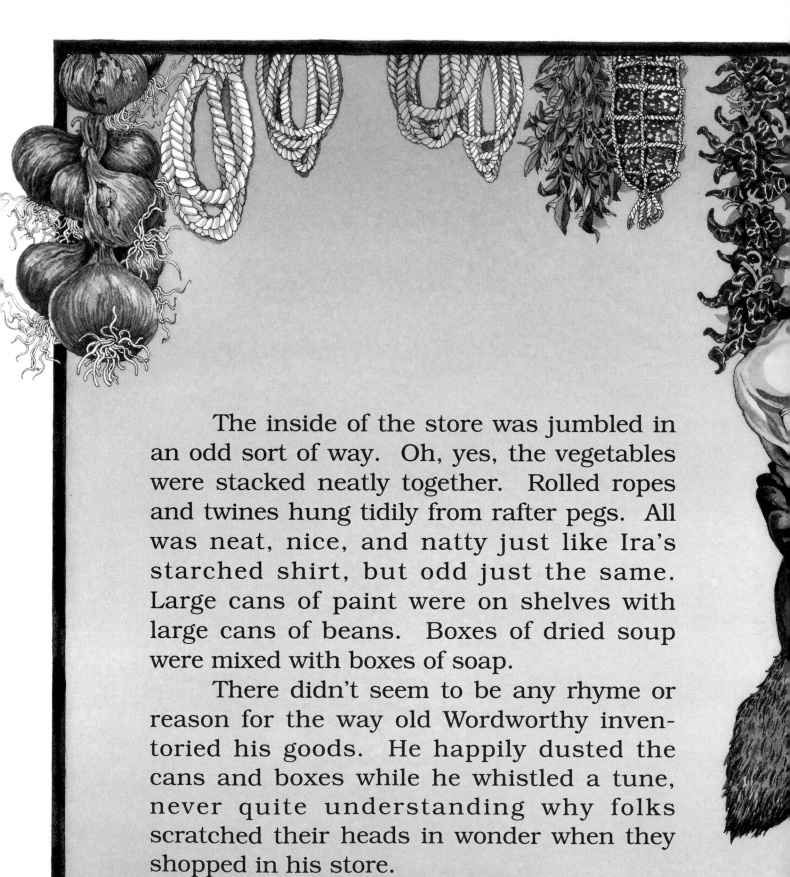

The inside of the store was jumbled in an odd sort of way. Oh, yes, the vegetables were stacked neatly together. Rolled ropes and twines hung tidily from rafter pegs. All was neat, nice, and natty just like Ira's starched shirt, but odd just the same. Large cans of paint were on shelves with large cans of beans. Boxes of dried soup were mixed with boxes of soap.

There didn't seem to be any rhyme or reason for the way old Wordworthy inventoried his goods. He happily dusted the cans and boxes while he whistled a tune, never quite understanding why folks scratched their heads in wonder when they shopped in his store.

But Wordworthy's Feed, Seed, and Mercantile was more than just a store; it was a meeting place, the center of all activity. It was a place where frumpy farmers could stand around and whistle in the wind about the weather and other wonders.

It was here, too, that the children of Barely There came after school to buy a soda or Sasparilla and giggle about those growing-up things. They would buy their drinks, and sometimes a persimmon or plum, and then sit on the boot-thumped steps and read a book from the library.

It was odd, but Ira didn't like the children sitting around on his steps. He didn't mind them drinking a pop or eating a plum, but it just plain bothered him that they sat around reading.

"Ahh . . . why can't they take their books and flip those pages someplace else?" he grumbled as he dusted the rows and rows of cans. "Books and learning are a waste of time; those kids should be learning a trade or mastering the fine art of farming," he fussed and fumed.

Finally, one day he could stand no more, and he stormed into the back room of the store. There he found paint, brush, and board, and with a mighty flourish he painted a sign—an important sign for things to come in Barely There.

He worked and worked for the longest time and finally, with a bit of paint splattered on his nose and eyeglasses, he whistled in satisfaction as he stood back and looked at his handiwork.

The next afternoon, just before school let out, he hung the sign on the porch outside. He bent a couple of nails in the process, but the sign was hung just the same.

When the school bell rang, the children, as was their wont, rushed to the store to buy their tasty treats. Ira stood and

watched, arms crossed, tapping a soft, furry foot on the porch. The children looked at him, looked curiously at the sign, then dashed inside.

One by one, as Ira glared, they grabbed and paid for their goodies. Then they zipped down the stairs and off to the meadows to read a bit and munch a bunch. Satisfied that the sign had done its duty, the crotchety old storekeeper went back inside.

The last of the children to leave the store was a shy little raccoon called Rita. The screen door squeaked and slammed as she stepped outside with an apple in her hand. She found a sunny spot on the stairs and there she sat down to read a book.

Ira's eyes opened angrily, opened wide, as he peered at her through the window from inside. There she was, first standing, now sitting below his fresh new sign, and he was sure Rita pretended she didn't see it.

"That girl must be blind," raged Ira as he stormed out the door. "Ahem," said he in a grumbling way, "maybe you didn't see the sign."

"Oh, yes, Mr. Wordworthy, sir," she replied in the sweetest of tones. "I saw the sign. It is very pretty."

"Pretty! Pretty indeed!" he roared as he tapped the sign with furry finger. "This sign says that all children of the younger persuasion are not to litter, loiter, or lay around here."

Then, to his shock and chagrin, little Rita looked up at the sign and quietly said, "No, it doesn't."

"Then, my little furry friend," he glowered, "just what does the sign say?"

Rita squinted her eyes and looked at the sign again. "It doesn't say anything."

Ira looked at the sign, squinting in concentration.

"Besides," added Rita, "why do you care if I sit on your porch and read a book?"

The little raccoon's gentle tone softened old Ira as his chin dropped to his chest, a small, stingy tear trickling from his eye. "Because I'm jealous," he truthfully said, "for I can't read nor write . . . nary a word, nary a letter."

Sure enough, if you looked carefully at the sign you would see that it was nothing more than squiggles, wiggles, and smears. It was very pretty, but it said nothing.

Every night thereafter, when the store was closed at half past dark, Rita sat in candles' flicker and taught Ira how to read and write. As time went on, the old badger learned to make his letters strong, and soon he could read to himself rather than being told.

The little raccoon loved playing teacher, and she would diligently grade his papers and listen intently as he read his lessons through and through.

From then and thereafter, Ira Word-worthy's store was a haven for children and their books. The mercantile became very organized as Ira learned to read the writing on his goods. He had known all the time that soap didn't go with soup; he just couldn't read the labels.

Oh, and that screen door squeaked and slammed all day long as children rushed in and out with sweets to eat and good books to read. Business was good, but Ira's mind was even better as he read book after book after book.

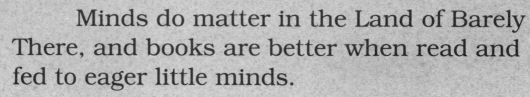

Minds do matter in the Land of Barely There, and books are better when read and fed to eager little minds.

Everything turned out pretty well, even though old Ira never quite learned how to spell . . .

in the Land of Barely There.